Unforgettable Travels: The Perfect Guide to Torquay 2025

Your Ultimate Passport to Torquay's Hidden Gems

Ava Dawson

Copyright © 2024 Ava Dawson

All rights reserved. No part of this publication may be reproduced, distributed, or transmitted in any form or by any means, including photocopying, recording, or other electronic or mechanical methods, without the prior written permission of the publisher.

TABLE OF CONTENTS

INTRODUCTION
- ❖ Welcome To Torquay: Why 2025 Is The Year to Visit
- ❖ How To Use This Guide
- ❖ Quick Facts and Torquay Travel Essentials

PLANNING YOUR TRIP TO TORQUAY
- ❖ When to Visit: The Best Seasons for Every Traveler
- ❖ Getting There: Transportation Tips and Tricks
- ❖ Accommodation Guide: From Luxury Hotels to Quaint B&Bs
- ❖ Packing for Torquay: Essentials for Every Season

EXPLORING TORQUAY'S FAMOUS ATTRACTIONS
- ❖ Living the Riviera Life: Torquay's

- Stunning Beaches
- ❖ The Iconic Marina: Boats, Boutiques, and Bayside Dining
- ❖ Historic Highlights: Torre Abbey, Kent's Cavern, and More
- ❖ Best Day Trips Around Torquay

HIDDEN GEMS AND LOCAL SECRETS

- ❖ Beyond the Tourist Trail: Secret Spots Only Locals Know
- ❖ Breathtaking Coastal Paths and Undiscovered Trails
- ❖ Hidden Cafés, Art Galleries, and Quaint Bookshops
- ❖ Unique Experiences: Private Tours and Secret Gardens

A FOOD LOVER'S GUIDE TO TORQUAY

- ❖ A Taste of the Coast: Top Seafood Restaurants
- ❖ The Café Culture: Local Coffee Spots You Can't Miss

- Traditional Dishes and Where to Find Them
- Nightlife and Wine Bars: Savoring Torquay After Dark

ADVENTURES IN NATURE

- Scenic Hikes and Walks: From Coast to Countryside
- Water Sports: Surfing, Kayaking, and Boat Tours
- Wildlife Watching: Local Flora, Fauna, and Nature Reserves
- Outdoor Escapes: Picnicking, Stargazing, and Hidden Beaches

TORQUAY FOR FAMILIES AND GROUPS

- Family-Friendly Attractions and Activities
- Best Beaches and Parks for Kids
- Group-Friendly Restaurants and Gathering Spots
- Planning for All Ages: Top Picks for

Everyone

ART, CULTURE, AND HISTORY
- Museums and Historical landmarks
- Art Galleries, Local Artists, and Cultural Centers
- Live Events and Festivals: A 2025 Calendar
- Walking Tours: Exploring Torquay's Storied Past

SHOPPING IN TORQUAY
- Unique Souvenirs and Local Crafts
- Boutique Shopping: Fashion, Home Decor, and More
- Farmers' Markets: Local Flavors and Handmade Goods
- Best Shopping Streets and Hidden Market Gems

WELLNESS AND RELAXATION IN TORQUAY
- Spas and Wellness Retreats

- Yoga, Meditation, and Mindfulness in Torquay
- Scenic Spots for Reflection and Relaxation
- Health-Conscious Cafés and Smoothie Bars

SUSTAINABILITY AND ECO-FRIENDLY TRAVEL

- Traveling Responsibly: Eco-Tips for Torquay Visitors
- Green Hotels and Restaurants To Support
- Ethical Wildlife and Nature Experiences
- How Torquay Is Going Green in 2025

APPENDICES

- Resources and Contacts
- Recommended Apps and Websites for Travelers
- A 2025 Calendar of Torquay's Annual

Events and Festivals
- Quick Language Guide: Local Phrases and Terms

CONCLUSION
- Wrapping up Your Torquay Adventure
- Staying in Touch with the Local Community
- Beyond Torquay: Exploring the English Riviera

INTRODUCTION

Welcome, traveler! You're about to plunge into Unforgettable Travels: The Perfect Guide to Torquay 2025, the must-have companion for experiencing the finest of Torquay!

Torquay, located on the magnificent English Riviera, is one of those coastal towns that has become a legend for good reason—think vast sandy beaches, charming hillside views, and a dazzling marina that just demands to be photographed.

In this book, we'll break down every must-see, uncover hidden gems only locals know, and provide you with everything you need to make your 2025 visit unforgettable.

Welcome To Torquay: Why 2025 Is The Year to Visit

If you've been thinking about visiting Torquay, let me inform you that 2025 is building up to be a fantastic year. Why? For starters, Torquay has gone above and above to provide guests with a more vibrant coastal experience. Over the last few years, the town's renowned landmarks have been thoughtfully upgraded, and new eco-friendly projects are making the area even more appealing to visitors looking to enjoy nature responsibly.

There are numerous reasons to make 2025 your year to explore this jewel, including the following highlights:

Nature Like Never Before

Imagine taking a morning stroll along pristine beaches with crystal-clear vistas, followed by an easy hike up to a clifftop viewpoint. Sounds good? Torquay has made significant progress in maintaining its natural beauty this year, with refurbished coastline paths and new viewing platforms that allow visitors to take in the breathtaking surroundings. Torquay's green spaces are currently at their finest, whether you're a seasoned hiker or just want to go for a casual walk.

Brand-New Attractions

Torquay has something new to offer everyone, from the renovated Torre Abbey with its bright art shows to new cultural sites across town. For example, the "Marine Life Encounter" project teaches you about local species (hello, playful seals!) while preserving their natural habitat. So, if you want unusual, interactive experiences, Torquay's new attractions will not disappoint.

Festival Galore

Torquay will host an increased calendar of events in 2025, including music festivals, outdoor film nights, and Devon-themed food markets. There's even a festival dedicated to Agatha Christie, Torquay's literary icon. Consider wandering around the streets while a live jazz musician performs, or having a fish & chips cone while admiring local artwork. Everything is happening this year.

Sustainable and Eco-Friendly Vibes

If you care about the environment (and who doesn't?) you'll appreciate Torquay's commitment to sustainability. More hotels are eco-certified, local restaurants are emphasizing zero-waste cooking, and electric bike rentals make it easier than ever to go without a car. When you visit Torquay in 2025, you will be part of a community that cares for the seaside.

In short, Torquay in 2025 offers the ideal combination of relaxation, adventure, and environmentally conscientious entertainment. It's all about making memories, whether with family, friends, or alone, while you sip a drink with a view of the sea and allow the fresh ocean wind to clear your mind.

How To Use This Guide

Let us make your Torquay adventure as simple and delightful as possible. Here's a breakdown of what you'll find in each area of this book and how to make the most of it.

Planning Your Trip to Torquay: Not Sure When to Go? We've broken down the ideal times to visit based on your travel taste (whether you prefer summer heat or fall foliage). This area includes transportation recommendations, packing lists, and even some local oddities to help you blend in as a visitor (or at least get a smile).

Exploring Torquay's Famous Attractions: This is where we go big. This section is packed with information about must-see attractions such as the Torre Abbey and the marina. We've got the inside scoop on the history, sights, and ideal photo angles.

Hidden Gems and Local Secrets - Want to venture off the main path? We've compiled a list of hidden gems, ranging from secluded eateries to less crowded cliffside walks.

Foodie's Guide to Torquay: Because, let's be honest, eating is an important component of any trip. We'll help you find everything from traditional fish and chips to seaside food that you can only get here.

Adventures in Nature: Torquay is more than just a beach destination! Hikers, kayakers, and wildlife enthusiasts will find this section useful for making the most of Torquay's natural wonders.

Art, Culture, and History: If you enjoy art, culture, and history, this is a must-see. We explore the art galleries, museums, and cultural events that bring Torquay's distinctive legacy to life.

And that's only a taste! Each section contains detailed advice, insider tips, and personal anecdotes from locals to help you make the most of your visit.

Quick Facts and Torquay Travel Essentials

Before you plunge in, here are a few requirements to ensure you're ready to face Torquay like a pro:

Weather: Torquay's pleasant, ocean-tempered climate means it is rarely too hot or chilly. Summers (June to August) are ideal for beach days, with highs about 70°F (21°C), and winters (December to February) are comfortable at around 50°F (10°C). Layers are your buddy, especially if you plan on taking evening walks by the sea.

Currency: The currency is the British pound (£). While credit cards are generally accepted, it is advisable to carry some cash, particularly for smaller vendors at markets and local shops.

Language: English (with a beautiful Devon accent). Don't worry if you don't know the local jargon; most people are kind and willing to assist you if you need directions or tips.

Transportation: Walking is one of the greatest ways to discover Torquay's charming streets, although buses and electric bikes are also popular options for further exploration. If you're looking for a rail trip along the shore, there are scenic coastal trains available.

Tipping: In restaurants, a 10-15% tip is customary if service is not included, however, tipping is not as common in cafes and bars. If in doubt, simply leave a tiny tip or a heartfelt "thank you!"

With this book in hand, you're all prepared to explore Torquay, find its beauty, and make memories that'll stay with you long after you've left its beaches. Are you ready to dive in? Let's go discover Torquay in 2025 style!

PLANNING YOUR TRIP TO TORQUAY

Welcome to the exciting portion of travel preparation! Planning a trip to Torquay is all about timing, transportation, and, of course, finding the ideal place to stay. I'll help you figure out when to travel, how to get there, where to stay, and what to pack so you're prepared for anything Torquay throws at you. Torquay has something for everyone, whether you want to relax on the beach, go on an adventurous coastal climb, or immerse yourself in culture.

When to Visit: The Best Seasons for Every Traveler

Spring (March-May): Torquay's springtime is simply stunning. Consider bright flower beds, refreshing beach breezes, and the first taste of sunshine after winter. During these months, the crowds are smaller, and the weather is usually moderate, with temperatures averaging 50-60°F (10-15°C).

It's an excellent time to walk along the cliffs, see gardens like Torre Abbey, and observe local wildlife as everything comes back to life. Spring is also when the English Riviera Flower Show begins, so if you enjoy flower displays, don't miss it!

Summer (June-August) is Torquay's peak season, and for good reason! The weather is ideal for beachgoers, with highs near 70°F (21°C). The beaches are crowded, the marina is full of boats, and the town comes to life with festivals, open-air concerts, and unlimited possibilities to swim.

It's an excellent time if you enjoy vibrant atmospheres, water activities, and bright days by the sea. Just be prepared for a few more people on the beach (hey, everyone wants a taste of paradise!) and book your accommodations in advance to get a good rate.

Autumn (September-November): Torquay's fall season is underappreciated, yet it's great for people who prefer a quieter, more scenic experience. The air cools significantly to around 50-60°F (10-15°C), which is ideal for scenic hikes and exploring the shoreline with fewer tourists around.

This season provides warm golden hues to the trees and a sense of tranquility. You might also catch the annual Torquay Seafood Feast, which features freshly caught fish and local delights. Fall is ideal for travelers who prefer a slower pace and a nice bar ambiance.

Winter (December-February): Although winter may not be the first thing that comes to mind when thinking of a coastal town, Torquay has a snug charm throughout the colder months. Temperatures rarely drop below 40°F (5°C), and many hotels and B&Bs provide special winter packages.

Imagine cuddling up in a charming café with a view of the sea, sipping a nice cup of tea, or taking tranquil winter walks along the cliffs. Winter is also when the town holds its seasonal markets, so it's ideal if you like holiday lights, mulled wine, and an off-season getaway.

Getting There: Transportation Tips and Tricks

Getting to Torquay is half of the fun, especially when you know your alternatives! If you're traveling from afar, it's easy to get there by train, automobile, or airline.

By Train: If you're traveling from London, take a direct train from Paddington Station to Torquay, where you'll arrive in approximately three hours. Trains also run from other important cities, including Bristol and Exeter. The views from the train are stunning, so grab a window seat if possible. You'll pass through rolling hills, coastal views, and green countryside—the ideal preview of what's to come.

By Car: Driving to Torquay allows you to explore nearby attractions such as Dartmoor National Park and other coastal towns. The trip from London takes roughly four hours. Just be prepared for some winding country roads as you approach closer; the sight is worth it, but tighten your seatbelts!

By Air: The nearest airports are Exeter (approximately 45 minutes away) and Bristol (about 1.5 hours). From there, you can easily rent a car or take the rail to Torquay. If you're feeling fancy, there are even helicopter services that provide spectacular flights down the shore!

Accommodation Guide: From Luxury Hotels to Quaint B&Bs

Torquay has a superb selection of places to stay, whether you want luxury, low-cost options, or something a little different.

Luxury Hotels: If you want to indulge yourself, stay at the Grand Hotel or The Imperial Torquay. These hotels are the epitome of grandeur on the English Riviera, equipped with spa facilities, pools, and accommodations that view the beautiful bay. Perfect for days when all you want to do is relax, have afternoon tea, or enjoy the scenery.

Boutique B&Bs: Torquay's boutique bed and breakfasts are difficult to beat for a warmer, more customized stay. Try the Cary Arms & Spa, which is almost located on the cliffs and offers breathtaking views of the sea from its rooms. Another favorite is The Somerville—think Victorian charm, breakfast produced with local ingredients, and owners who have lots of recommendations to make your stay particularly special.

Budget-Friendly Stays: If you're trying to save a bit, Torquay has plenty of pleasant, reasonable options. Many family-run guesthouses and smaller hotels offer great deals, especially if you book in advance. Premier Inn Torquay is a dependable alternative that won't break the budget while also keeping you close to the major attractions.

Unique Stays: For something out of the ordinary, consider coastal cottages, eco-lodges, or even a restored lighthouse! Sites like Airbnb and Vrbo provide tons of entertaining and unique accommodations where you may enjoy a more local experience.

Packing for Torquay: Essentials for Every Season

The good thing about Torquay's climate is that it's generally mild, so you don't need to dress differently for each season. However, there are a few necessities you should keep on hand.

Spring and fall are perfect for layering. Consider light sweaters, a comfortable scarf, and a jacket that can withstand a gust of wind or a passing drizzle. You will want to explore the coastal walks, so bring a pair of good walking shoes.

Summer: Bring swimsuits, a beach blanket, and sunscreen. Even while it is not tropically hot, the sun may be intense when you are out by the ocean. A sunhat and sunglasses will be your finest companions. Comfortable sandals or light sneakers are ideal for beach days and wandering around town.

Winter: Although it rarely gets cold, you'll need a heavy coat, especially for evening excursions along the coast. A raincoat or waterproof garment is particularly useful because winter might bring the odd downpour. And, of course, bring comfy clothes to curl up in cafes!

Year-Round Essentials: Regardless of the season, always bring a reusable water bottle (hydration is essential for coastal walks!), a portable phone charger (for all those shots), and a small backpack to keep your hands free while exploring. And if you enjoy reading, bring a nice book. Nothing beats a couple of pages featuring an ocean vista.

With your vacation planned, you're ready for an amazing stay in Torquay!

EXPLORING TORQUAY'S FAMOUS ATTRACTIONS

Welcome to the heart of the English Riviera. Torquay's allure is an intoxicating combination of natural beauty, ancient history, and seaside pleasure. Torquay has something special to offer, whether you want to relax on the beach, explore ancient caves, or learn about intriguing history. This section contains information on the top attractions in Torquay, as well as day trips to adjacent South Devon jewels.

Living the Riviera Life: Torquay's Stunning Beaches

Torquay's beaches are among the finest in England. Soft dunes, turquoise waters, and majestic cliffs make each one feel like a small paradise. Here are a few must-see destinations to begin your Riviera adventure:

Torre Abbey Sands: Located in the heart of Torquay, this beach features golden sands and a lengthy promenade ideal for seaside strolls. Torre Abbey Sands is quite popular in the summer, and there's a reason for that! Whether you're a sunbather or a swimmer, this beach offers the ideal balance of relaxation and action. Grab an ice cream and enjoy the traditional English coastal atmosphere.

Oddicombe Beach: For those who want a somewhat more rugged beauty, this is the place to go. Oddicombe is renowned for its distinctive red cliffs and sheltered bay. It's a little quieter than Torre Abbey Sands, which makes it great for anyone trying to avoid the throng. Fun fact: there's a funny little cliff railway here that takes you up and down the slope, so if you're not up for a tough climb, take the Babbacombe Cliff Railway for a ride with spectacular views.

Meadfoot Beach: This beach is more private, with a pebbly shoreline and a rocky backdrop. Meadfoot is a local favorite for kayaking and snorkeling due to its clean waters and rich marine life. If you are an early riser, consider going here for sunrise—it is certainly worth it.

Each beach has a distinct personality, so why not make it a goal to visit them all? Just remember to bring sunblock, a good book, and perhaps a beach towel to recline in true Riviera style.

The Iconic Marina: Boats, Boutiques, and Bayside Dining

The marina is a must-see for anybody visiting Torquay. It's the town's pulsing center and an excellent location for people-watching, boat-gazing, and savoring the freshest seafood. Walking along the promenade, you'll notice everything from fancy ships to small fishing boats floating in the ocean. The marina exudes a wonderful vitality, especially in the evening when the lights reflect off the water, creating a magical atmosphere.

Top Marina Activities:

Boutiques and Shops: The marina area is brimming with boutique boutiques selling anything from beachwear to handcrafted items. One of the most lovely boutiques is a little nautical-themed gift shop on the main pier. You may find souvenirs, sea-salt-scented candles, and even a traditional fisherman's sweater if you're feeling very coastal.

Bayside Dining: Dining near the water is essential. For fish enthusiasts, consider The Elephant, Torquay's only Michelin-starred restaurant that uses fresh, locally sourced foods. For a more relaxed meal, visit Harbour Kitchen, which serves some of the greatest fish & chips around. Pro tip: if possible, get an outdoor seat because nothing goes better with fish and chips than a cool sea wind and a view of the water.

Boat Tours and Cruises: If you want to venture beyond the marina, many boat tours provide journeys along the coast, dolphin-spotting excursions, and sunset cruises. If you're feeling adventurous, some places even offer snorkeling excursions. Seeing the shoreline from the water is an entirely new experience, and with a little luck, you might glimpse a friendly seal or even dolphins playing in the surf.

Torquay Marina is a must-see for those looking to shop, dine, or simply enjoy the views. It's one of those places that immediately makes you feel like you're on vacation.

Historic Highlights: Torre Abbey, Kent's Cavern, and More

Torquay is more than simply beaches and shopping; it also has a rich history. From prehistoric caves to historic estates, history fans will find lots to explore.

Torre Abbey, which dates back to 1196, is a beautiful monastery with an interesting history. The monastery itself is full of historical antiques and art exhibitions, while the grounds are a haven of color, complete with exotic flora and even a "potent garden" with medicinal herbs!

This restaurant feels like a trip back in time, yet with a modern twist. Agatha Christie, Torquay's most renowned resident, spent time here as a child, and the gardens include an area dedicated to her famous detective, Hercule Poirot.

Kent's Cavern: Enter the Stone Age at Kent's Cavern, one of Britain's oldest prehistoric sites. More than 500,000 years ago, early people lived in these caverns. A guided tour will take you deep into the caves, where you'll witness old rock formations, fossils, and possibly even some friendly bats. The guides are lots of fascinating anecdotes, so don't be shocked if you leave feeling like you've traveled back in time to the age of woolly mammoths!

Agatha Christie Mile: Torquay honors its famed mystery writer with the Agatha Christie Mile, a self-guided walking tour of her favorite places. You'll explore locations such as the Grand Hotel, where she spent her honeymoon, and the Princess Gardens, which inspired scenes in her novels. It's an enjoyable way to explore Torquay while following in the footsteps of a legend.

These historic features provide an excellent balance to your beach time, allowing you to connect with Torquay's rich history.

Best Day Trips Around Torquay

If you want to go beyond Torquay, numerous day-trip alternatives highlight the best of Devon's landscape and coastline.

Dartmoor National Park: Located just a 40-minute drive away, is a breathtaking landscape of rolling hills, ancient stone circles, and wild ponies. It's an ideal location for hiking, picnics, or simply taking in the pure rural air. Dartmoor is ideal for those who enjoy stunning views and wide-open landscapes.

Paignton: Torquay's neighbor and another coastal beauty is only a 15-minute drive or train journey away. Paignton Zoo, a Victorian pier, and even a steam railway provide trips through the gorgeous South Devon landscape. It's a family-friendly destination with plenty to see and do.

Brixham: A lovely fishing resort with a short drive or ferry ride from Torquay. Brixham, known for its colorful harbor and working fishing fleet, is ideal for both seafood lovers and photographers. Do not miss the replica of Sir Francis Drake's famed ship, the Golden Hind, which is anchored right in the harbor.

Exeter: Roughly 40 minutes distant and offers a taste of metropolitan life. Exeter features a strong arts scene, a historic cathedral, and a variety of boutique shops. It's an excellent day excursion if you want to experience history and culture with an urban touch.

Each of these destinations lends a distinct flavor to your Torquay visit, giving you a better sense of Devon's different landscapes and experiences.

Torquay provides plenty of options to make amazing memories, whether you're lazing on the beach, discovering old caves, or strolling through historic neighborhoods. So grab your camera, pack your sunscreen, and prepare to discover the best of the English Riviera!

HIDDEN GEMS AND LOCAL SECRETS

If you want to venture beyond the typical tourist attractions in Torquay, you're in for a treat. While the popular beaches, marina, and Torre Abbey are fantastic, most people seldom see the other side of Torquay.

From secret coastal walks and tucked-away eateries to one-of-a-kind experiences that capture the essence of this town, this section is dedicated to the hidden treasures and local secrets that make Torquay genuinely remarkable.

Beyond the Tourist Trail: Secret Spots Only Locals Know

One of the finest elements of any trip is discovering hidden gems that only locals know about, and Torquay is no exception.

Here are a few hidden gems that may not be on everyone's agenda, but are well worth a visit.

Elberry Cove: A secret beach in Paignton with a pebbly coast and crystal-clear water. It's only accessible by foot, which keeps the crowds at bay, making it ideal for a relaxing afternoon. The cove is surrounded by old stone ruins that were formerly part of a medieval bathhouse. If you want to take a dip, it's also an excellent snorkeling location!

Anstey's Cove: Another hidden gem, Anstey's Cove is like a private slice of paradise. It's a calm, secluded beach surrounded by limestone cliffs, and the water is crystal blue, giving it the feel of a mini-Mediterranean retreat. The trek down the cliff path is half of the experience (and a bit of a workout), but once there, you can relax on a deck chair and enjoy the peace.

Beacon Cove: A short walk from the main harbor, this little cove is popular among locals, particularly families looking to avoid the crowds. It is nestled away near the Living Coasts region, so most visitors miss it entirely. Bring a picnic and lay a blanket for a private, intimate view of the water. It's also a great site to see the sunset!

These locations are ideal for anyone seeking quiet and nature—just remember to carry your swimwear, sunscreen, and perhaps a good book to read by the lake.

Breathtaking Coastal Paths and Undiscovered Trails

Torquay's coastline is overflowing with breathtaking views, and while certain roads are well-traveled, there are a few hidden gems that provide something truly unique. These trails are perfect if you're looking for some adventure (and don't mind a few hills along the way).

The South West Coast Path to Maidencombe: This lesser-known section of the South West Coast Path leads you through breathtaking cliffs, wildflower fields, and secluded coves. It's a little difficult in sections, but the vistas are worth it. At Maidencombe Beach, you can reward yourself with a quick dip or simply relax and enjoy the scenery. This walk is also a photographer's delight, with each curve offering a fresh beautiful picture of the shoreline.

Babbacombe Downs to Oddicombe Beach: This is a quieter portion of Torquay's shore, leading from Babbacombe Downs through forested pathways to Oddicombe Beach. You'll walk through shaded glens and along cliff-top paths that provide panoramic views of the English Channel. Plus, there's a secluded seat about halfway down that's ideal for catching your breath and admiring the scenery.

Watcombe to Maidencombe Coastal Walk: This route is a local favorite, with calm paths winding along the cliffs and through the forest. The trail eventually leads to the isolated Watcombe Beach, where you can take a break and possibly see some local species. It's best to go with decent walking shoes and a sense of adventure, but the vistas are amazing, especially around daybreak.

These trails provide the ideal blend of Torquay's natural beauty, away from the people. Bring snacks, and a camera, and be prepared to get some sand on your shoes!

Hidden Cafés, Art Galleries, and Quaint Bookshops

After a day of exploring, there's nothing better than finding a warm place to relax.

Torquay has plenty of quaint cafes, hidden art galleries, and charming booksellers that make ideal pit stops.

Small World Café: This small retreat in the heart of Torquay has the greatest coffee in town and a pleasant atmosphere. Locals enthuse about their baked cakes (the lemon drizzle is a standout), and there's usually a continuous stream of polite customers. The café provides a pleasant, domestic atmosphere, with mismatched furnishings and bookcases stocked with titles to peruse while sipping.

Artizan Gallery: Located down a quiet alley, Artizan Gallery is a refuge for art enthusiasts. The gallery's shows, which feature local artists, vary regularly, so there is always something fresh to view. From contemporary paintings to elaborate sculptures, it's a visual feast. In addition, the gallery has a nice garden in the back where you can sit and relax with a cup of tea.

The Book Stop: There's something magical about a small, independent bookstore, and The Book Stop in Torquay is exactly that. With shelves stacked high with everything from classic novels to obscure travel guides, it's easy to get lost in here. The proprietor is also a wealth of local knowledge and can gladly recommend a good beach book. Keep an eye out for the "local history" section—there are some fascinating facts about Torquay's past lurking there!

Unique Experiences: Private Tours and Secret Gardens

Torquay has several surprises in store for anyone seeking a one-of-a-kind experience. Whether it's a private tour with a knowledgeable local or a calm escape to a secret garden, these experiences add a magical touch to your journey.

Private Walking Tours with a Local Guide: Torquay has a fascinating history, and there's no better way to discover it than on a private walking tour led by a knowledgeable local. Guides frequently take you off the main road to locations like the oldest parts of town, hidden alleys, and sites associated with renowned residents such as Agatha Christie. You'll hear stories that you wouldn't find in a guidebook, making it a genuinely unique way to discover Torquay.

The Secret Garden at Cockington Court: Although Cockington Court is well-known for its lovely grounds and craft studios, there is one hidden gem here: the Secret Garden. It's a beautiful little getaway hidden behind ivy walls, complete with meticulously maintained flower beds, shaded chairs, and even a little pond. It's the ideal location for a quiet picnic or to simply relax in nature's embrace.

Berry Head National Nature Reserve: Just a short drive from Torquay, has stunning coastline vistas and is a great site to watch wildlife. Locals consider it an excellent site for birdwatching, and if you're lucky, you might even view dolphins or seals from the cliff edge. The routes are simple to follow, and there's a comfortable café with breathtaking views at the top—perfect for replenishing after a lovely climb.

From tucked-away gardens to secret beaches and lovely eateries, Torquay's hidden gems and one-of-a-kind experiences will make your trip unforgettable. So, take a detour, follow a less-traveled path, and see a side of Torquay that most people miss.

A FOOD LOVER'S GUIDE TO TORQUAY

Welcome to Torquay, where seaside flavors combine with local characters to create a dynamic and wonderful food scene! Torquay has something for everyone, whether you enjoy seafood, coffee, or just a fantastic night out. From fresh fish and chips by the sea to snug cafés and bustling wine bars, this guide will help you find the town's best eats.

Prepare to eat your way around the English Riviera, with recommendations, tips, and personal experiences to make your culinary journey as memorable as possible.

A Taste of the Coast: Top Seafood Restaurants

Torquay knows how to provide seafood. With the English Channel lying at its doorstep, the town's eateries can get some of the freshest fish and shellfish in the UK. Here are some of the best places to eat Torquay's finest seafood.

The Elephant: Let's start with the big one! The Elephant is Torquay's sole Michelin-starred restaurant, and it focuses on fresh, locally produced cuisine. Their seafood meals are a true celebration of seaside flavors, with a unique twist that keeps customers returning. The menu changes seasonally, but if lobster or seared scallops are available, don't hesitate! It's a bit of a splurge, but it's well worth it, and you can eat while overlooking the marina.

No. 7 Fish Bistro: Tucked away in the port, No. 7 is a relaxed, family-run seafood restaurant that prioritizes quality. The atmosphere is welcoming and unpretentious, and the cuisine speaks for itself. The mussels and grilled fish platters are local favorites, and the amounts are generous. Make sure to reserve a table—this hidden gem fills up quickly!

Rockfish: If you want classic fish and chips with a twist, this is the place to go. Located right on the waterfront, they provide responsibly sourced seafood with sea views. What's better than crispy fish and golden chips served with a helping of fresh sea air? For a creative twist, try their curry sauce—it's really tasty and lends a distinct flavor to the typical dish.

Every dish at these establishments provides a flavor of Torquay's bustling beach lifestyle. Also, remember to bring a napkin for the inevitable tartar sauce splash. It is all part of the experience!

The Café Culture: Local Coffee Spots You Can't Miss

Torquay boasts a lovely assortment of cafés that cater to individuals who enjoy starting their day with a warm coffee and a friendly atmosphere. Whether you enjoy a flat white or a traditional cappuccino, these shops will not disappoint.

Velo Coffee: This is a local favorite, tucked away in a quiet spot near the waterfront. The café features a casual, cycling-inspired design and serves some of the best coffee in town. Their baristas are knowledgeable about the beans, and the quality shines through in every cup. Plus, the pastries are fresh, flaky, and ideal for breakfast. Try the almond croissant with a cappuccino; you will not be disappointed.

Me and Mrs. Jones: If you're looking for a fashionable spot with good coffee, Me and Mrs. Jones is your place. Torquay's trendy tiny café has a modern decor and an artistic spirit that makes it feel like a slice of London. Their espresso drinks are excellent, and their avocado toast goes well with a morning brew. And if you're lucky, you might be able to get a place by the window for some excellent people-watching.

Calypso Coffee Company: Ideal for those looking for a beachy, relaxed ambiance. It's directly on Babbacombe Road and near the shore, so you can grab a coffee before or after a walk down the beach. Their iced lattes are extremely refreshing on a hot day, and they offer a good assortment of sandwiches for a quick lunch. Friendly service and bright design give this establishment a warm, inviting atmosphere that is difficult to resist.

These cafes are ideal for a relaxing morning or an afternoon pick-me-up. Simply add a nice book, a buddy, or a few peaceful moments to yourself, and you've got the recipe for the ideal coffee break in Torquay.

Traditional Dishes and Where to Find Them

No vacation to Torquay would be complete without trying some traditional English cuisine. While there is lots of international diversity here, you should sample a few local meals to get the complete experience.

Cream Tea at Angels: Angels in Babbacombe serves Devon's famous cream tea. Consider this: a warm scone smeared with thick clotted cream and a spoonful of sweet jam. Yes, it's just as good as it sounds! What is the best part? You may enjoy this English classic while sitting outside on a bright day with views of the seaside.

Pasties at The Pasty House: While Cornwall is known as the birthplace of the pasty, Torquay also has some great variations. The Pasty House offers a variety of cuisines, including conventional beef and potato and vegetarian options like cheese and onion.

These golden, flaky pockets make a great quick lunch or snack on the run, and they're surprisingly filling.

Sunday Roast at The Hole in the Wall: The Hole in the Wall pub serves a delicious, traditional Sunday roast. Picture a platter packed high with roast beef, crunchy potatoes, Yorkshire pudding, and gravy. It's the ultimate comfort dish and an excellent way to sample the flavors of a traditional English Sunday.

From sweet cream teas to savory pasties, Torquay's traditional snacks are a must-try.

Nightlife and Wine Bars: Savoring Torquay After Dark

Torquay's nightlife scene has something for everyone. Whether you're searching for a nice wine bar, a boisterous tavern, or a place to dance, the town comes alive after sunset with alternatives for every taste.

Below Decks: This beachside pub and restaurant transforms into a pleasant nightly destination with live music, delicious cocktails, and breathtaking views. Below Decks, located on the port, is an excellent place to start the night. Grab a drink, settle in for some live music, and let the seaside wind create the mood for a relaxing evening.

Cary Arms & Spa: For a more refined experience, Cary Arms provides an intimate atmosphere with an extensive wine selection and well-made drinks. Perched on the cliffside, the views are stunning, especially around sunset. It's a bit of a hidden gem for a refined evening, ideal for a romantic date or quiet drink.

The Wine Box: A must-see for wine enthusiasts. This intimate pub serves an outstanding assortment of wines from all around the world, as well as local alternatives from Devon wineries. The staff is informed, and they will gladly assist you in selecting anything that meets your preferences. If you want to try a variety of wines, they also have wine flights available.

The Apple & Parrot: For a more relaxed night out, The Apple & Parrot is a busy pub with a terrific vibe. They frequently have live music and events, so expect a lively crowd and positive feelings. Try their local ciders, which bring a Devon flavor to the conventional pub experience.

Torquay's nightlife offers enough to offer for a wonderful night out, whether you're drinking wine with friends, dancing to live music, or enjoying a beachside cocktail.

Torquay is a foodie's dream, with the best seafood restaurants and charming cafes, as well as traditional specialties and a lively nightlife. So bring your appetite and curiosity, for this coastal town is ready to provide some unique culinary experiences!

ADVENTURES IN NATURE

Torquay excels in combining coastal beauty with endless outdoor adventures. This location is for everybody who wishes to immerse themselves in nature, not simply those who enjoy sunbathing and coastal strolls.

Torquay's natural playground is yours to explore, whether you want to go on a picturesque stroll with breathtaking views, participate in exhilarating water sports, or spend a quiet afternoon in a secret area with only the birds and waves for company.

Grab your walking boots, picnic basket, or even a wetsuit, and let's explore Torquay's wild side!

Scenic Hikes and Walks: From Coast to Countryside

Let's start with one of the best ways to experience Torquay's landscapes: hiking. This area has some of the most beautiful walking trails, and there's something for everyone, from casual walkers to experienced trekkers.

Here are several hikes and walks that will allow you to experience Torquay's natural beauty firsthand.

The South West Coast Path: This is the trail that rules them all, spanning along the English Riviera and providing some genuinely beautiful views. The stretch from Torquay to Babbacombe is a must-do, snaking along the cliffs with the turquoise water below. Every bend brings a fresh view—craggy cliffs, flowery fields, and secret coves. The path is signposted but be prepared for some ups and downs. It's a workout, but it's worthwhile.

And who doesn't want a good excuse to have an extra scone afterward?

Cockington Country Park: For a softer walk, visit Cockington Village. You'll feel like you've walked into a postcard, complete with thatched-roof homes and horse-drawn carriages. The park itself features lovely forest trails and rich gardens that are ideal for a relaxing stroll. Pack a picnic, find a shady area, and spend a relaxing afternoon admiring the tranquil beauty of the English countryside.

Berry Head National Nature Reserve, just a short drive from Torquay, provides both history and nature. The seaside path here is breathtaking, with panoramic views of the sea and, if you're lucky, dolphins frolicking in the waves beneath. The area is also a birdwatcher's delight, with peregrine falcons swooping overhead. The vistas are most beautiful during sunrise and sunset, so plan your visit around those times.

Water Sports: Surfing, Kayaking, and Boat Tours

Torquay's crystal-clear seas beckon water enthusiasts. From surfing to kayaking, there are numerous ways to get up close and personal with the ocean. Here are some of the most effective techniques to make an impression in Torquay.

Kayaking at Babbacombe Bay: If you've never tried sea kayaking, Babbacombe Bay is an excellent place to begin. The water here is quiet and clean, making it ideal for both beginners and experienced paddlers. You can rent a kayak or take a guided excursion along the cliffs and into secluded coves that are inaccessible on foot. What is the best part? The chance to see seals playing in the waves—they're surprisingly curious and might come up beside your kayak to say hi!

Surfing at Goodrington Sands: While Torquay isn't Hawaii, it offers a good surf environment, particularly for novices. Goodrington Sands is an excellent beach for trying out the waves, with surf schools available for those interested. Imagine riding a wave, refreshing sea spray on your face, and views of the English coast all around. And, yeah, you may fall off, but that's half the fun!

Boat Tours and Wildlife Cruises: For a more relaxed trip, embark on a boat tour from Torquay Harbour. These excursions take you out along the coast, providing a unique view of the cliffs, beaches, and bays. There are also dedicated wildlife tours where you can see dolphins, seals, and a variety of seabirds. Bring your camera and keep an eye out—the wildlife here is full of surprises.

Wildlife Watching: Local Flora, Fauna, and Nature Reserves

Torquay and the adjacent Devon coastline support an astonishing variety of flora and fauna. Whether you're a devoted birder or simply appreciate taking a stroll through nature, there's lots to see and explore.

Berry Head National Nature Reserve: As previously indicated, Berry Head is a popular destination for wildlife enthusiasts. This protected region is home to unique plant species, seabird colonies, and the elusive Greater Horseshoe Bat. It's an excellent bird-watching location, with gulls, razorbills, and, if you're lucky, peregrine falcons. Grab a pair of binoculars and see how many species you can spot.

Occombe Agricultural & Nature Trail: A great day out for families, Occombe Farm blends wildlife and agricultural life. The nature walk leads through woodlands and meadows, where you can see native flora and watch butterflies and bees. Kids will like viewing the farm animals, and there is even a farm shop where you can purchase some local delights to take home.

Babbacombe Cliff Gardens: For those who prefer a less strenuous nature experience, the Babbacombe Cliff Gardens provide a calm escape with lovely, well-maintained floral arrangements. It's a nice place to enjoy the splendor of the seaside without going too far. Furthermore, the grounds provide stunning views of Babbacombe Bay—bring your camera!

Outdoor Escapes: Picnicking, Stargazing, and Hidden Beaches

Sometimes all you need for a beautiful day is a blanket, a tasty snack, and a stunning view.

Torquay has plenty of great settings for a peaceful outdoor vacation.

Picnicking at Meadfoot Beach: Meadfoot Beach is a modest but picturesque location with views of the cliffs and blue waters below. There's plenty of room to spread out a blanket and enjoy a picnic. Bring some local cheese, a fresh baguette, and perhaps a bottle (or two) of cider, and spend the afternoon in the sun.

Berry Head is a great place to stargaze because of its low light pollution. The headland juts out into the sea, providing unimpeded views of the night sky. Pack a warm blanket, and a thermos of hot chocolate, and set out for an evening of stargazing. If you're lucky, you may see a shooting star or two.

Elberry Cove: For those seeking a little more privacy, Elberry Cove is a secret beach only accessible on foot. With its rocky shore and beautiful, welcoming water, it's an excellent place for swimming and snorkeling. The tranquil environment and natural beauty make it feel like your own personal slice of heaven.

Torquay has a wide range of outdoor activities to satisfy every style of nature lover, from coastal hikes and exhilarating water sports to peaceful picnics and stargazing nights. So pack your hiking boots, grab your snorkel, and get ready to create some wonderful experiences in Torquay's natural playground.

TORQUAY FOR FAMILIES AND GROUPS

Torquay excels in making families and groups feel at home. With so much to do, it's the perfect destination for everyone, whether they're traveling with children, teenagers, or friends looking to build memories together. Torquay boasts an unlimited range of activities to keep everyone happy, from sandy beaches great for castle building to fascinating museums and fun-filled parks.

Family-Friendly Attractions and Activities

Torquay boasts many family-friendly attractions where everyone can have fun. The attractions here combine adventure and learning, keeping everyone happy.

Living Coasts Zoo & Aquarium: Begin with a visit to the popular Living Coasts, which combines a zoo and an aquarium to provide an entertaining experience for both children and adults. Kids enjoy seeing penguins up close (who doesn't?), and you can even observe feeding times for some of the resident creatures. Something is amazing about seeing seals and sea lions play just feet away. Believe me, the smile on your children's faces will be priceless!

Kents Cavern: For families who enjoy combining adventure and history, Kents Cavern is a must-see. These ancient caves are filled with interesting rock formations and stories from early human history. The trip is kid-friendly, with just the perfect amount of mystery and thrill, and the guides are fantastic at engaging young minds. My niece still discusses her "cave explorer" experience to this day! And, let's be honest, there's something immensely amazing about traveling underground to see where early humans lived.

Torquay's Dinosaur World is a hands-on museum with life-size dinosaur models, interactive exhibitions, and fossil-digging activities that will enthrall young visitors. It's a little odd but in the greatest manner imaginable. It's difficult to say who had more fun here: the youngsters or the grownups pretending to know everything about T-Rex and the triceratops.

Best Beaches and Parks for Kids

Torquay is all for its beaches, and happily, several are suitable for families. You have sandy beaches, shallow waters, and plenty of places to relax while the kids play. Here's where you may enjoy some sun, the beach, and make amazing memories.

Goodrington Sands: This beach is great for families because of its golden sands and calm waves that are wonderful for paddling. Goodrington Sands also has a waterpark nearby, so if the kids get bored of the sand (unlikely, but possible), there are slides and pools for more splash-filled fun. Bring a bucket and spade—this is an ideal sandcastle area!

Babbacombe Beach: Nestled in a gorgeous cove, Babbacombe Beach is a bit quieter and ideal for families wishing to relax. The kids can wade in the shallow waves, and there is a café right on the beach where they can have a snack or an ice cream cone to keep everyone happy. Furthermore, the view from the cliffs is breathtaking, making it a must-see for both parents and photographers.

Cockington Court and Country Park: Cockington Country Park, located a short distance from the town center, is reminiscent of a fairytale. The children will enjoy exploring the lovely gardens, feeding the ducks in the pond, and roaming along the woods trails. Horses and small houses add to the lovely atmosphere. Don't miss the craft center, where you may take home unique gifts to remember the day.

Group-Friendly Restaurants and Gathering Spots

Torquay offers a variety of dining alternatives that accommodate families and larger groups. Whether you want a quick nibble, a conventional pub meal, or something a little more special, you can find it here.

Rockfish: A family favorite, Rockfish is located right next to the harbor. It is well-known for its fresh fish and chips, and the welcoming atmosphere makes everyone feel at ease. There are lots of kid-friendly alternatives (such as small fish and chips), and adults may enjoy a range of local seafood. Plus, nothing beats the view of the port while dining—it's a terrific place to relax and watch the boats come and go.

The Hole in the Wall: This is one of Torquay's oldest pubs, full of character, and offers a welcoming atmosphere for both large groups and families. The menu includes everything from hefty pies to traditional Sunday roasts, as well as kid-friendly options such as chicken nuggets and noodles. It's snug, welcoming, and charming—the perfect place to unwind after a day of activity.

The Elephant Brasserie: For groups looking for a special treat, The Elephant provides an excellent dining experience with a menu based on local foods. It's a little more upmarket, yet it caters to families and groups. The cuisine here is amazing, and the views of the marina make it much better. Just make sure to reserve in advance because it's a popular spot.

Planning for All Ages: Top Picks for Everyone

Torquay is a place where everyone may find something they enjoy. To make preparation easier, here are some top options for different age groups.

For the Little Ones (Ages 3-7): Younger children will enjoy the Living Coasts Zoo & Aquarium interactive displays and the opportunity to see animals up close. Goodrington Sands beach is especially suitable for small children, thanks to its shallow waters and soft sand, which are perfect for endless digging and castle building. Dinosaur World, of course, is popular with children who enjoy dinosaurs.

For Tweens and Teens (Ages 8-16): Teens and tweens seeking more adventure will enjoy Kent's Cavern and its historical interest. The South West Coast Path has breathtaking views and routes for older children who enjoy hiking. For some excitement, try renting a kayak or paddleboard at Babbacombe Beach—ideal for adventurous teenagers looking to explore.

For the Whole Family: Cockington Court & Country Park is suitable for all ages, with lovely gardens, craft stores, and open areas to run or rest. Rockfish and The Hole in the Wall are both fantastic family eating options, with diverse menus to suit everyone's tastes.

For Adults: If you're traveling with other adults, consider stopping at Berry Head Nature Reserve. The rocks and fauna here are breathtaking, and it's a tranquil area for a scenic walk. Cary Arms & Spa is another excellent choice for a bit of luxury and relaxation, with breathtaking vistas and a friendly atmosphere.

Torquay is a place where everyone can get together and have a good time, thanks to its various family-friendly and group-friendly activities, beaches, and food options. Torquay has something for everyone, whether you want to explore nature, relax on the beach, or try some wonderful local cuisine. Prepare to pack your luggage, collect your loved ones, and embark on an unforgettable family vacation!

ART, CULTURE, AND HISTORY

Welcome to Torquay, where history, art, and culture merge as naturally as the waves do with the shore. This picturesque seaside town is more than simply beautiful vistas and beach days; it has a rich, colorful history that awaits exploration, as well as a vibrant arts culture that caters to everyone.

Torquay's cultural scene is worth exploring, with iconic landmarks, must-see museums, local art galleries, and an intriguing festival planned for 2025. Let's take a look at Torquay's story to understand what makes it unique.

Museums and Historical landmarks

Torquay is peppered with historical sites that narrate stories from antiquity to the current day. These museums and sites serve as open pages in the town's history book, revealing stories of prehistoric humans, famous authors, and Victorian beauty.

Torre Abbey Museum: Begin with a visit to Torre Abbey, Torquay's oldest structure, dating back to 1196. Originally a monastery, it has subsequently been renovated into a museum and art gallery where visitors may experience medieval and Victorian life. The grounds here are breathtaking, with exotic flora, sculptures, and even a medieval herb garden. If you're a history enthusiast (or simply enjoy a nice photo opportunity), the Abbey's magnificent architecture and rich gardens are a must. I recall my first visit, feeling like I was in a BBC drama set centuries ago!

Kent's Cavern: In terms of ancient history, Kent's Cavern is one of Europe's most notable prehistoric caverns. These caves, which were once inhabited by early humans, include interesting rock formations and archaeological artifacts. Guided tours take you through the caves, which include traces of ancient human existence stretching back 500,000 years! Imagine standing where our forefathers once did, gazing at the same stone formations. It's surreal and rather humbling.

Agatha Christie Mile: Mystery fans rejoice! Torquay is Agatha Christie's hometown, and she is widely celebrated there. The Agatha Christie Mile is a walking track that takes you to numerous spots linked with the "Queen of Crime." Beginning at the Princess Pier and passing past the Grand Hotel (where she spent her honeymoon), it's a delightful opportunity to learn about Christie's life and career. Pro tip: get a map and follow the path, picking up trivia along the way. Even if you're not a mystery enthusiast, it's a pleasant stroll down Torquay's stunning seafront.

Art Galleries, Local Artists, and Cultural Centers

Torquay's art scene is dynamic and diversified, with galleries featuring established and upcoming artists. This is a town that values creativity, and you'll find plenty of local talent on show. If you want to see Torquay via an artistic lens, these galleries and organizations are excellent choices.

Artisan Gallery: This intimate, community-focused gallery is a favorite among art enthusiasts, with a rotating schedule of exhibitions by local artists. There are modern paintings and sculptures, as well as conventional seascapes and abstract pieces. The gallery features an intimate and warm atmosphere that encourages visitors to interact with the artists' work. Keep an eye on their events schedule, since Artizan frequently conducts meet-the-artist evenings and seminars.

Cockington Court Craft Studios: Nestled within the charming Cockington Village, Cockington Court houses a variety of craft studios. Glassblowers, potters, jewelry makers, and others demonstrate their skills here. It's a great spot to get a one-of-a-kind souvenir or simply watch artisans at work. Glassblowers attract both children and adults as they make intricate pieces directly in front of their eyes. Visiting here is like going back in time, with artists crafting stunning, handcrafted artifacts in such a historic location.

Torquay Museum: Torquay Museum offers a combination of art, history, and the occasional unusual display. It's a remarkably eclectic museum with everything from ancient Egyptian items to Agatha Christie exhibits and an intriguing fossil collection. If you are traveling with children, they will like the interactive exhibitions. It's also an excellent rainy-day choice, with plenty to see indoors, including the history of the English Riviera and its cultural evolution over time.

Live Events and Festivals: A 2025 Calendar

Torquay's festival scene is brimming with excitement, particularly in 2025, which promises to be a year jam-packed with music, food, art, and culture. Whether you're here for a weekend or a week, these events can make your stay even more exciting.

Torbay Royal Regatta (August): This yearly event is a must-see, with boat races, live music, and fireworks over the bay. It's a great family event that gives the area a lively vibe. Locals and visitors congregate at the waterfront to cheer on the contestants and enjoy the festive atmosphere. The regatta is a

Torquay institution that dates back over 200 years—talk about history!

Agatha Christie Festival (September): This event is for fans of the great novelist. The Agatha Christie Festival features themed events such as murder mystery dinners, literary seminars, and vintage fairs. Imagine dressing in your best 1920s clothing and immersing yourself in the world of Poirot and Miss Marple among other admirers. Whether you're a voracious reader or just here for the experience, it's a real delight.

Brixham Pirate Celebration (May): A short drive from Torquay, this family-friendly celebration transforms Brixham into a pirate paradise. People from all around attend dressed in their finest pirate attire, and the town is alive with live performances, reenactments, and plenty of "are!"If you have children, they will enjoy dressing up and joining in on the pirate fun.

Walking Tours: Exploring Torquay's Storied Past

Walking through a town can be the greatest way to experience it, and Torquay has many tours that bring its history to life. Walking tours allow you to get up close and personal with Torquay's sights while learning about the interesting stories that have shaped the town's identity.

Torquay Ghost Tour: Want to experience the eerie side of Torquay? This ghost tour is a popular evening excursion that takes you through the darkest periods of town history. With tales of haunted houses, spooky encounters, and mystery people, it's ideal for everyone who enjoys a good ghost story. You'll discover hidden alleys and back streets you'd never locate on your own, with a guide who understands how to send shivers down your spine.

The Historic Torquay Walking Tour is a more traditional trip that visits significant sights such as Torre Abbey and the Royal Terrace Gardens. It's an excellent chance to learn about the town's Victorian history, its role in the creation of coastal resorts, and notable individuals such as Agatha Christie. The guide's personal experiences and anecdotes give a warm, friendly atmosphere to the trip.

Cockington Village Heritage Walk: If you're willing to venture outside of town, the heritage walk around Cockington Village is well worth it. This picturesque, postcard-perfect village is rich in history, with thatched cottages, antique stone structures, and quaint craft studios. The guide brings the village's history to life, telling anecdotes of old families, local traditions, and how Cockington has kept its beauty for decades.

Torquay's cultural side is as rich and welcoming as its coastal views, with art galleries full of local talent and historical tours that take you into the heart of the town. It's a site where you may learn about medieval history and current art, enjoy a bustling festival, or simply meander through the alleyways, discovering treasures with each step. So be ready to enjoy the sights, sounds, and stories of Torquay, a town that is both lovely and vibrant.

SHOPPING IN TORQUAY

If you believe that shopping is as important as sightseeing when traveling, you've come to the correct place. Torquay is known for more than just its beaches and stunning landscape; it also has a plethora of unique stores, lovely markets, and craftsmen selling one-of-a-kind items.

Torquay's shopping culture offers something for everyone, from handmade goods and eccentric boutiques to farmer's markets brimming with local tastes. Prepare to stroll, shop, and take home a small piece of the English Riviera.

Unique Souvenirs and Local Crafts

Let's begin with the essentials: souvenirs. The days of bringing back the usual postcard or keychain are over (though we all secretly love them). Torquay boasts an excellent range of one-of-a-kind, handcrafted products that make ideal keepsakes or gifts. Several pieces show the town's coastal charm and artisan flair.

Cockington Court Craft Studios: Located just a short distance from Torquay's town center, Cockington Court is a magical, must-see destination. Artists and craftspeople make anything from handcrafted jewelry and pottery to blown glass and woven textiles. Strolling through the artisan studios is like entering a mini-art village. You're likely to meet some of the artists themselves, and many are eager to talk about their work. On my last visit, I observed a glassblower produce a tiny, glittering fish—it was a truly remarkable experience!

Agatha Christie-inspired Gifts: Torquay is the birthplace of Agatha Christie, the Queen of Crime, so it's only natural that there are various businesses dedicated to her legacy. Shops sell mystery novels, vintage trinkets, and even witty T-shirts or tote bags featuring phrases from her books. These make excellent gifts for any bookworm or wannabe detective in your life.

Driftwood Creations & Nautical Décor: The handcrafted driftwood art and nautical home décor offered at various outlets represent Torquay's distinct seaside ambiance. Driftwood picture frames, candle holders, and wall art create lovely, rustic souvenirs for your beach vacation. I couldn't resist taking home a driftwood frame, which now houses one of my favorite beach images!

Boutique Shopping: Fashion, Home Decor, and More

If you enjoy boutique shopping, Torquay has you covered. With its eclectic mix of independent retailers and lovely boutiques, you'll find unusual apparel, one-of-a-kind home decor products, and all the small touches that make shopping here so enjoyable.

Mint Dress Agency: Known for its selected range of high-end and designer clothes, is a hidden gem for individuals who enjoy browsing premium apparel without paying exorbitant rates. This boutique offers a constantly changing selection of trendy clothes and sophisticated accessories. It's ideal for a quick splurge or simply browsing. They frequently have vintage stuff, so you might come across a timeless classic with a story behind it.

SoHo Living: This boutique has become a popular destination for home decor enthusiasts. SoHo Living is a great combination of furniture, fashionable home decorations, and adorable little knick-knacks that you didn't realize you needed but couldn't live without. The mood is effortlessly stylish, with a coastal flare that reflects Torquay's personality. It's an excellent location to find something both beautiful and utilitarian, such as a throw cushion, a unique lamp, or a pair of beach-themed coasters.

Bygones Old Emporium: Part museum, part shop, Bygones is a quirky wonderland of old treasures. Items available here range from Victorian knick-knacks to weird historical artifacts. It's a trip back in time, and you'll most certainly lose track of time while exploring its treasures. I once discovered an old-fashioned pocket watch that my grandfather enjoyed, proving that Bygones has something for everyone!

Farmers' Markets: Local Flavors and Handmade Goods

Torquay's farmers' markets offer local cuisines and artisan goods that highlight the best of Devon's countryside. Whether you're looking for freshly baked croissants, artisan cheeses, or handcrafted soaps, these markets provide a real experience of the region.

Torquay Farmers' Market: Held every Thursday on the main high street, this farmers' market is an excellent place to buy local produce and artisan delicacies. You'll discover stalls selling fresh fruits and vegetables, handcrafted pies, and local jams. If you're a foodie, don't miss the cheese kiosks, which offer anything from velvety blue cheese to mature cheddars created just down the road. Furthermore, the scents are incredible—imagine fresh bread, pastries, and sizzling bacon!

Occombe Farm Shop: For a more permanent market atmosphere, travel to Occombe Farm. This farm shop is stocked with locally sourced and organic produce. It's the type of location where you can sample the flavors of Devon, with honey, jams, and chutneys prepared by local suppliers. There's also an on-site café where you can sit and enjoy a genuine cream tea (remember, in Devon, jam comes first, then cream!).

Made in Devon: This little market appears around town throughout the year, with artisans and small companies offering everything from hand-poured candles to hand-knitted scarves and blankets. The items are all labeled "Made in Devon," so you know you're receiving a genuine local item. It's the ideal place to support small companies while bringing home something truly unique.

Best Shopping Streets and Hidden Market Gems

Torquay's main retail lanes are a mix of well-known stores and independent boutiques, but if you know where to look, there are also hidden market jewels to be discovered.

Fleet Street is a bustling shopping district that includes everything from high-street names to independent stores. Shops like White Stuff and FatFace offer casual attire that complements Torquay's beach ambiance. Take a stroll down Fleet Street to discover classic favorites, but keep an eye out for any undiscovered gems in between.

Union Square Shopping Centre: If you prefer a more traditional shopping experience, Union Square includes a wide range of retailers, from fashion and beauty to bookstores. It's an excellent place to fill up on necessities or get any last-minute trip supplies.

Harbour Market: A delightful seasonal market located right by the marina, Harbour Market is a great area to promote while buying locally manufactured goods. Artists sell paintings, jewelers show off beach-inspired designs and even a few food carts are providing fresh munchies. There's something lovely about exploring local crafts with the sea in the background—it's a genuine Torquay experience.

St Marychurch Precinct: This beautiful little district is a more relaxed shopping destination, with independent boutiques selling anything from crafts to baked goodies. It has an old-world vibe and is ideal for escaping the town center's bustling population.

Torquay's shopping culture has something for everyone, from farmers' markets and crafts to sophisticated boutiques. Each street and store has its personality, capturing the essence of this lovely seaside town. So grab your tote bag, put on some comfortable shoes, and prepare to take a piece of Torquay home with you.

WELLNESS AND RELAXATION IN TORQUAY

When you think of Torquay, you might imagine sunny beaches, crystal blue waters, and possibly Agatha Christie writing her next mystery. But did you know Torquay is also an excellent destination for wellness and relaxation? Torquay has something for everyone, whether you enjoy spa treatments, yoga, or simply want to relax by the sea.

With world-class spas, gorgeous meditation locations, and health-conscious cafés to nourish your body and mind, it's the ideal place to unwind. Are you ready to find your beachside zen? Let's dive in.

Spas and Wellness Retreats

Nothing says "vacation" like a spa day, and Torquay has plenty of options for pampering.

Consider this: you're lounging by a peaceful pool, the quiet hum of the waves in the background, and you're covered in a fluffy robe. Doesn't that sound dreamy? Torquay's spas and health retreats offer all you need to unwind, refresh, and possibly even glow a little!

The Imperial Torquay Spa: One of the most iconic relaxing destinations, The Imperial offers breathtaking views of the English Riviera. Their spa offering ranges from exquisite massages and facials to detoxifying body wraps. I had their seaweed wrap once (it felt very mermaid-like), and it was the perfect reward after a day of exploration. They also feature an indoor and outdoor pool, so you can choose your preferred atmosphere. Even if you only have a few hours, visiting The Imperial seems like a mini-vacation.

Cary Arms & Spa: This boutique spa provides a unique "beach hut" experience—yes, you read that correctly! Cary Arms' spa huts, located directly by the sea, give a pleasant, rustic vibe while still providing high-quality services. You may arrange a full spa day, including a massage and facial, and then relax in their hydrotherapy pool overlooking the sea. Can it get any more coastal-chic? Their treatments incorporate natural, local ingredients that leave you feeling completely revitalized.

Beyond Escapes Devon: About a 20-minute drive from Torquay, Beyond Escapes is ideal for those seeking a more isolated atmosphere. Their spa specializes in holistic therapy, offering both traditional treatments and one-of-a-kind experiences such as the "Aqua Thermal Suite," which features heated loungers and saunas. If you're searching for a complete retreat, they offer wellness packages that include a cottage, spa services, and even yoga sessions.

Yoga, Meditation, and Mindfulness in Torquay

Torquay's sea air virtually beckons you to calm down, take a deep breath, and find your center. Torquay provides a few fantastic options for individuals who enjoy yoga or meditation or who wish to try it for the first time.

Yoga by the Beach: Every summer, local instructors lead beach yoga sessions directly on the water. There's nothing quite like doing yoga to the sound of waves as your music. Most courses are beginner-friendly, so even if you're new to yoga, you can easily participate. Plus, stretching on the sand as the sun rises above the water? It's a lovely way to begin any day.

Maddy's Yoga Studio: Located in the town center, Maddy's Yoga Studio is a pleasant environment that provides a variety of programs, including Vinyasa and gentle restorative yoga. Maddy has a talent for making everyone feel at ease, and the studio has a welcoming, casual vibe. They also offer meditation and mindfulness workshops, which are ideal for deepening your understanding of these techniques. I once took a meditation lesson here and left feeling more peaceful than I had in years.

Hatha Yoga Torquay: Hatha Yoga, another local favorite, provides courses for all skill levels. They are well-known for their small class sizes and personal approach, making it ideal for those seeking a more private experience. Many of their programs emphasize physical and mental relaxation, with a focus on breathing techniques and soft positions.

Scenic Spots for Reflection and Relaxation

Sometimes all you need to unwind is a gorgeous view and some quiet time to yourself. Fortunately, Torquay has plenty of lovely sites ideal for introspection and relaxation.

Royal Terrace Gardens (Rock Walk): For a calm spot with breathtaking views of the seashore, climb the steps of Rock Walk. This terraced garden has wonderful views of Tor Bay and is an ideal spot for a stroll, reading a book, or simply watching the waves flow in. In the evening, the lights create a magical environment, making it ideal for calm reflection.

Anstey's Cove: If you prefer a more private setting, Anstey's Cove is a hidden treasure of a beach that feels worlds away from the busy town center. It's small, quiet, and surrounded by cliffs, making it ideal for a solo walk or a relaxing meditation session. Bring a blanket, sit on the rocks, and enjoy the fresh sea air. On my last visit, I spent the afternoon here, listening to the water and watching kayakers pass by. Bliss.

Babbacombe Downs: This cliffside promenade offers some of Torquay's best vistas. Take a leisurely walk around the Downs and find a bench to sit and enjoy the scenery. On a clear day, you can see as far as Exmouth. It's a popular hangout for both locals and visitors, and the serene setting is excellent for some meditation or quiet thought.

Health-Conscious Cafés and Smoothie Bars

Wellness and relaxation go hand in hand with delicious food, and Torquay has lots of options to keep you energized and rejuvenated. Here are a few places to have a healthful meal, ranging from smoothie bars to health-focused cafés.

The Green Leaf Café: This quaint café in the town center serves a variety of healthy, plant-based meals. From superfood-packed smoothie bowls to hearty vegetarian wraps, everything on the menu is fresh and delicious. They also serve delicious herbal teas and juices. I couldn't resist sampling their avocado toast, which was topped with pomegranate seeds and a sprinkle of seeds—a bright and tasty delight!

Viva Smoothies is Torquay's go-to place for smoothies, smoothie bowls, and freshly squeezed juices. They serve a selection of nutrient-dense smoothies, including classic green blends and energetic berry-based alternatives. Their smoothie bowls are edible works of art, adorned with vibrant fruit, granola, and even edible flowers. If you're looking for something refreshing and healthful, this store has you covered.

The Kind Grind: Located near the waterfront, The Kind Grind specializes in vegan and gluten-free options that do not sacrifice taste. Their matcha lattes and turmeric golden milks are perfect for warming up on a cold day, and they also offer a great assortment of raw and vegan delicacies. I once tried their chocolate peanut butter slice, and let's just say I'm still dreaming about it.

Occombe Farm Café: Just a short drive from town, Occombe Farm is an organic farm and café that provides locally produced food. Their menu is seasonal and health-conscious, providing something for everyone, including vegetarians and gluten-free customers. It's a terrific place to grab a healthy breakfast or lunch before exploring the farm's nature paths.

Torquay's health services are diverse and lovely, whether you're looking for a spa day, a sunrise yoga session by the sea, or simply a peaceful place to contemplate. So, take a deep breath, allow the sea breeze to work its magic, and enjoy the gentler pace of the English Riviera. Torquay is here to help you relax, refuel, and leave with a sense of peace that will last long after your visit.

SUSTAINABILITY AND ECO-FRIENDLY TRAVEL

When visiting a wonderful location like Torquay, it's natural to want to help keep it as beautiful as you found it. Fortunately for us, Torquay is working hard to make it easy to be a good traveler, with green projects cropping up everywhere.

From eco-friendly hotels and restaurants to nature-friendly activities and basic eco-tips, this guide will help you travel responsibly, allowing you to fully appreciate Torquay's beauty with peace of mind. Let's look at how you may be a green traveler while still having an amazing time on the English Riviera.

Traveling Responsibly: Eco-Tips for Torquay Visitors

Being an eco-conscious tourist does not require you to change all of your habits; minor changes can add up! Here are some useful eco-friendly suggestions to remember throughout your Torquay journey.

Pack a reusable bag, water bottle, and coffee cup: These are the holy grail of environmentally friendly travel gear. Torquay has many stores, cafés, and markets, so bringing a reusable bag will come in handy. When it's time for coffee or tea, use your reusable cup instead of a single-use one! Many Torquay coffee shops even provide a small discount if you bring your cup, so your commitment to the environment may save you a few pennies.

Take Advantage of Torquay's Excellent Public Transportation: Torquay's buses, trains, and scenic ferry routes make it easy to explore without a car. The Torquay-to-Brixham ferry is a beautiful, scenic alternative that lowers your carbon footprint. Furthermore, if you're up for it, Torquay's shoreline is fairly accessible, with plenty of picturesque sites to discover on foot or by bike. Walking reduces emissions, allows you to travel at your own leisure, and allows you to uncover hidden gems that you might otherwise overlook!

Respect Nature (No Picking Wildflowers!): It's tempting to pluck a wildflower or two for a keepsake, but those delicate ecosystems rely on everything remaining in balance. Instead, snap images to preserve the memory and ensure that Torquay's wild places remain attractive for future visitors. On walks, stick to marked routes, and when picnicking, leave no trace (except perhaps a positive vibe for the next people).

Green Hotels and Restaurants To Support

Torquay offers a variety of accommodations and dining alternatives that go above and beyond to safeguard the environment. Here are some eco-friendly hotels and restaurants that prioritize sustainable practices:

The Cary Arms & Spa: Known for its sustainability efforts, The Cary Arms minimizes its environmental impact through energy-saving measures and local food and material sources. The rooms are constructed with environmentally friendly elements, and the spa even employs natural, locally derived goods. They're dedicated to decreasing plastic use, and their coastal views make it clear why they care about the water!

The Imperial Hotel: In addition to providing an unforgettable stay, this historic hotel has adopted environmentally responsible measures in its operations. They've introduced several energy-saving initiatives, such as smart lighting and water-saving techniques, and they source the majority of their food locally, reducing transportation emissions. The hotel's beachfront location indicates that they are particularly committed to sustainability efforts, which makes being here feel wonderful in more ways than one.

Occombe Farm Café: A short drive from the town center, Occombe Farm Café is a great place for breakfast or lunch, and their commitment to sustainability is outstanding. Their food is locally produced and organic, and they work to limit waste and plastic consumption. After your dinner, you can take a walk around the farm's nature trails, which are kept sustainably to safeguard local species.

Green Leaf Café: For a more relaxed, environmentally friendly dining experience, Green Leaf Café offers plant-based cuisine that is both delicious and sustainable. The café stresses local products and offers a variety of vegan and vegetarian cuisine to cater to all dietary choices. Their smoothies and salads are a must-try, and the laid-back environment makes it an ideal place to unwind and enjoy a fresh meal.

Ethical Wildlife and Nature Experiences

One of the most tempting aspects of visiting Torquay is discovering its natural beauty, which ranges from rough shorelines to wildlife-rich places. Here's how to enjoy these events while being environmentally conscious.

Living Coasts Coastal Zoo: This coastal zoo and aquarium focuses on conservation and education, assisting in the protection and rehabilitation of marine species. Their dedication to sustainability includes breeding programs for endangered species and educating visitors about the importance of ocean health. Visiting Living Coasts benefits local and global conservation efforts while also making learning about marine life interesting and enjoyable.

Guided Nature Walks and Wildlife Tours: Many of Torquay's nature tours are led by guides who value ethical techniques, ensuring that local wildlife is protected and environments remain intact. From bird-watching walks to rock pool tours around the coast, these guides are passionate about Torquay's natural beauty and take care to leave it in the same condition they found it. Joining one of these excursions will not only provide you with a wealth of knowledge but will also help to support eco-friendly tourism initiatives.

Berry Head National Nature Reserve: Located just outside Torquay, Berry Head is a beautiful reserve where you can go trekking, bird viewing, and even see seals in the waters below. The reserve takes conservation seriously, with a focus on safeguarding the cliffs and the wildlife that live there. Visitors are asked to stay on the paths and avoid disturbing the wildlife, making it an excellent area to enjoy nature without harming the ecosystem.

How Torquay Is Going Green in 2025

Torquay is pushing up its environmental efforts, and 2025 is shaping up to be a green year for the town. Torquay is embracing new measures to conserve the environment and keep the town lovely for years to come, as it places a greater emphasis on sustainability.

Reducing Single-Use Plastics: Torquay has made a concerted effort to minimize single-use plastics in recent years, with numerous cafés, restaurants, and retailers joining the cause. This year, you'll notice more reusable options, such as bamboo cutlery and paper straws. Refill stations are also cropping up around town to encourage guests to fill up their water bottles without purchasing plastic.

Clean-Up Initiatives: Torquay's local government has worked with community groups and volunteers to undertake regular beach and park cleanups. Visitors are always welcome to participate in these activities, which are both enjoyable and meaningful ways to give back while enjoying the outdoors. It's a tiny effort that makes a huge difference, and the more the merrier when it comes to keeping Torquay's beaches clean.

Green Transport Options: Torquay has enhanced its public transportation choices and provided additional electric vehicle (EV) charge spots throughout town as part of its efforts to reduce automotive pollution. The town is attempting to make its infrastructure more bike-friendly, and many hotels provide bike rentals to encourage visitors to explore the area on two wheels.

Eco-Education Programs: Torquay has created various community programs to raise awareness about sustainable practices, allowing both locals and tourists to participate. These activities range from sustainable culinary seminars to hands-on conservation efforts, allowing anybody to learn and assist in Torquay's transition to a greener future.

Whether you're drinking a smoothie with a bamboo straw, strolling along a beach maintained by volunteers, or staying at a green hotel, every small effort toward sustainability helps Torquay remain the gorgeous coastal hideaway it is today.

By adopting eco-friendly travel behaviors, you not only make a good influence but also form a deeper connection with the location you're visiting. So, let's do our lot, embrace the greener side of travel, and keep Torquay gleaming for future generations.

APPENDICES

Welcome to the final part of your Torquay trip guide! Here's where we gather all of the necessities to make your journey as seamless and enjoyable as possible.

This appendix is your ultimate arsenal for making the most of your time on the English Riviera, including useful resources, contact information, and a schedule of local events.

So, grab a notebook (or open your notes app), because this section will help you feel like a local and keep organized as you discover everything Torquay has to offer.

Resources and Contacts

Whether you're creating an emergency contact list or simply need a quick answer about transportation or weather, here are some key contacts and resources to have on hand.

Torquay Tourist Information Centre: A wealth of maps, brochures, and informed people waiting to answer your queries. Located in the heart of town, this is the place to go for in-depth local knowledge and help with bookings or guided tours.

- Phone number: +44 1803 211211.
- Website: English Riviera.

Local emergency numbers:

- Emergency services (police, fire, ambulance): 999.
- Non-emergency medical assistance (NHS 111): 111
- Torbay Hospital: +44 1803 614567.

Transportation:

- Stagecoach Bus Service (local buses): +44 1392 427711.

- Torquay Train Station (for schedules and tickets): National Rail, +44 3457 484950
- Torquay Taxis: For a quick lift, contact local services such as Devon Taxis or Torbay Taxis.

If you're out and about and need some recommendations or a friendly face, Torquay's small stores, cafés, and eateries are typically happy to help or share local knowledge.

Recommended Apps and Websites for Travelers

Apps and websites can be unsung heroes in ensuring a seamless travel experience. Here are a few to download or bookmark before heading out:

Trainline provides real-time train schedules and ticket buying. The software makes it simple to keep track of your train journeys, particularly if you're planning day trips from Torquay.

The Stagecoach Bus App covers local bus routes, provides real-time arrivals, and even enables mobile ticket transactions. Useful if you're visiting Torquay and want to travel like a local.

Visit South Devon App: A virtual guidebook to Torquay and the surrounding areas, with recommendations for sights, eating, and forthcoming events. It's like having a tour guide right on your phone!

Google Maps is the classic for a reason! Google Maps can help you navigate Torquay's meandering roads and beaches, and you can save spots to visit later.

Eventbrite: This app is particularly handy for Torquay's annual festivals, as it frequently includes ticket information and schedules for local events.

WhatsApp is used by many locals and small enterprises in the United Kingdom. It's also useful for connecting with other travelers or tour groups.

A 2025 Calendar of Torquay's Annual Events and Festivals

Torquay enjoys a good celebration, and there are plenty of festivals and events to attend throughout the year. Here's an early glimpse at what's coming up in 2025, so you can plan your vacation around something fantastic!

Torquay Food & Drink Festival (March): A gastronomic wonderland! Torquay's food festival highlights local chefs, restaurants, and suppliers. Expect cooking demonstrations, cuisine tastings, and the opportunity to sample Torquay's best fish & chips. Bring your hunger!

English Riviera Literature Festival (April): Ideal for bookworms, this yearly festival brings together authors, writers, and readers to celebrate literature. With guest talks, book signings, and workshops, it's a fantastic event to attend.

Brixham Pirate Festival (May): Arguably one of the region's liveliest festivals, the Brixham Pirate Festival is held just down the coast from Torquay. Expect pirate-themed parades, costume contests, and plenty of live music. Feel free to embrace your inner pirate!

Torquay Regatta (August): A long-standing event, the Torquay Regatta features water sports, sailboat races, and family activities. There is also a spectacular fireworks display over the port.

Fishstock Brixham (September): Celebrating Torbay's fishing legacy, Fishstock is a seafood lover's paradise. This is one of the year's most delicious events, with fresh-caught seafood, live bands, and cookery demonstrations.

Agatha Christie Festival (September): Torquay, Agatha Christie's hometown, commemorates the famed novelist with a mystery and intrigue festival every September. Fans of Christie's novels will enjoy the themed events, murder mystery dinners, and walking tours based on her life and work.

Christmas by the Sea (December): Nothing compares to the charm of the festive season on the English Riviera. Christmas markets, festive lights, and caroling fill the air with joy, making December an ideal month to visit Torquay.

Quick Language Guide: Local Phrases and Terms

While Torquay inhabitants speak English, you may hear some local slang or British terminology that is unusual. Here is a simple guide to help you fit in!

"Cream tea" is a must-try in Torquay! Cream tea is tea served with scones, clotted cream, and jam. But be warned: the Devonian approach is to put on the clotted cream first, then the jam!

"Sarnie": An informal word for a sandwich. So, if someone offers you a "cheese sarnie," accept and have a fantastic snack!

"Lovely jubbly" is a happy term that indicates something is outstanding. For example, after experiencing your first cream tea, you may say, "Lovely jubbly!"

"Cheers" is a polite way to express thank you that is not limited to clinking glasses. If a local provides you instructions or answers a query, a simple "cheers" will make you sound like a local.

"**Mooch**" is a term used to describe a casual walk around town. You might hear a local say, "Just going for a mooch around the shops," which means they intend to browse or stroll without a specific destination.

"**The English Riviera**" refers to the Torbay area (Torquay, Paignton, and Brixham), which is famous for its gorgeous beaches and sunny weather. Calling it "The Riviera" is very Torquay-like!

"**Knackered**": When you hear someone say "knackered," it suggests they are fatigued. After a day of visiting Torquay, you'll be exhausted!

"**Chuffed**" signifies pleased or cheerful. So, if you're having a fantastic time in Torquay, you may say you're "chuffed to bits!"

"Grockle": Some locals use the term "grockle" to refer to tourists in a lighthearted way. If you're out on the seaside with your camera, you might hear, "Look at the grockles enjoying the beach!"

"Mind the gap": You'll probably hear this aboard trains, urging passengers to be aware of the space between the train and the station. It's one of those classic British phrases that's difficult to forget!

With these tools, recommendations, and local knowledge, you'll be ready to make the most of your time in Torquay. Whether you're arranging your trip around a festival, conversing with people in their language, or traveling like a pro, you'll fit in and create memories that feel more like a local experience than a tourist one. Here's to a terrific 2025 in the English Riviera!

CONCLUSION

So here we are at the end of your Torquay voyage, and what a ride it has been! Whether you've been entranced by magnificent seaside sunsets, discovered hidden jewels in twisting alleyways, or indulged in one too many cream teas (don't worry, there's no judgment here), your time in Torquay is sure to leave you with unforgettable memories.

Let's revisit the magic of Torquay, offer a few methods to stay connected with its community, and take a look beyond this delightful town to see more of the English Riviera.

Wrapping up Your Torquay Adventure

Torquay has the feel of a loving welcome from a long-time friend. You've enjoyed its sunny beaches, walked along the renowned marina, and marveled at historic sites such as Torre Abbey and Kent's Cavern. Not to mention all the unexpected encounters – whether you met a kind local who directed you to a secluded beach, or you discovered a café that feels like a home away from home. These small discoveries are what make Torquay such a memorable place.

Torquay's unique feel includes a relaxed pace, lively bars, and salty sea air that whispers, "Just one more day..." Each region, from hectic commercial districts to calm coastline pathways, has its personality, and you've undoubtedly figured out which one feels most like you. There's no doubt that you'll leave with more than just photographs. You'll leave with stories to share for years.

Staying in Touch With the Local Community

Just because you're leaving does not mean you have to say goodbye completely. Torquay residents like staying in touch with visitors who have discovered the town's beauty. Here are a few ways to stay connected and bring some of Torquay with you wherever you go:

Social Media: Follow local hotspots, artists, and community organizations on social media. Many Torquay establishments, including attractive cafés, bustling bars, and even local artists, have an active web presence. Not only will this allow you to view familiar persons and locations from a distance, but you may also notice announcements for events and festivals that may inspire your next visit!

English Riviera Newsletter: Sign up to get the English Riviera tourism email. This way, you'll receive notifications about the latest events, special travel recommendations, and seasonal activities right in your inbox. It's like getting a small piece of the coast in your email every month.

Join Local Groups: If you've met some local acquaintances, inquire about joining community groups or forums online. People can stay engaged by following local Facebook pages or Instagram and WhatsApp groups. It's a great way to maintain friendships and stay up to date-on anything Torquay.

Beyond Torquay: Exploring the English Riviera

If your adventures in Torquay left you wanting more, the English Riviera has you covered. Torquay is only one of the magnificent seaside towns that make up this region, and each one has its distinct shine.

Here are a few local sites worth visiting on your next trip:

Paignton, located just a short distance from Torquay, has something for everyone. It's family-friendly, with sandy beaches ideal for paddling, a historic pier, and Paignton Zoo, where you can interact with exotic creatures. Paignton is a great blend of coastal enjoyment and easygoing charm.

Brixham: This fishing town is ideal for anyone who enjoys the colorful coastal life. Brixham is famous for its bustling harbor, a recreation of Sir Francis Drake's ship, and delicious seafood at every turn. Stroll around the shoreline, admire the colorful architecture, and eat some of the greatest fish & chips around. If you want a good time, the Brixham Pirate Festival in the spring is a must-see!

Cockington Village: If you're looking for something a little more charming, Cockington Village is like going back in time. This beautiful community, located just a short drive from Torquay, is home to thatched houses, art studios, and picturesque gardens. It's the ideal place to unwind and take in the tranquil scenery.

Dartmoor National Park: For those seeking adventure, Dartmoor is a dream come true. Dartmoor, with its wild, rocky terrain, old stone circles, and infinite walking routes, contrasts sharply with Torquay's beach attractiveness. Hiking here is an experience you'll remember long after your vacation.

Exploring beyond Torquay brings up a new world of discovery, and each town on the English Riviera has something special to offer. So, while planning your next trip, consider it "Torquay, Take Two," and set aside time to explore the region's other attractions.

Parting Thoughts

The fun of travel is discovering locations that leave an impression on you, and Torquay has a way of doing just that. As you reflect on your time on the English Riviera, remember the sensation of sandy beaches underfoot, the sound of laughter ringing from the marina, and the sight of colorful boats bobbing in the bay. Torquay will be waiting for you whenever you decide to return. And, until then, keep those memories near, share your stories, and keep an eye on those travel newsletters for the most recent updates from your favorite coastal getaway. Safe travels, and here's to Torquay, the town you'll always return to. Cheers!

Made in United States
North Haven, CT
04 May 2025

68563504R00075